The Fullness of God

The Fullness of God

Ankia van der Merwe

Copyright © 2011 by Ankia van der Merwe.

ISBN: Softcover   978-1-4568-3578-1
           Ebook   978-1-4568-3579-8

All rights reserved. No part of this book may be reproduced or transmitted in any form or by any means, electronic or mechanical, including photocopying, recording, or by any information storage and retrieval system, without permission in writing from the copyright owner.

This book was printed in the United States of America.

To order additional copies of this book, contact:
Xlibris Corporation
0-800-644-6988
www.xlibrispublishing.co.uk
Orders@xlibrispublishing.co.uk

Contents

Introduction 9

Chapter 1: The Lord God 13

Chapter 2: The Lord, Jesus Christ 29

Chapter 3: The Lord our Father 38

Chapter 4: Holy Spirit 42

Chapter 5: Manifestations of the Holy Spirit 58

Chapter 6: Fruit of the Spirit 73

Chapter 7: The Fullness of life 84

I would like to thank my Lord Jesus and the Holy Spirit
for giving me the opportunity and time to write this book.
Thank you to my husband, Hannes and
my children, Joané, Elminda & Handré
for their support and patience.
I would like to thank my family & friends
who prayed with me and supported me to
be able to get this book published.
I appreciate all your love and support!
May you be blessed.

Love you all,

Ankia

It is my prayer for you that as you read this book:

"that you may really come to know practically, through experience for yourselves, the love of Christ, which far surpasses mere knowledge without experience; that you may be filled through all your being unto all the fullness of God, may have the richest measure of the divine Presence, and become a body wholly filled and flooded with God Himself! Eph 3:19

Introduction

How many Christians can say that they experience the fullness of God in their lives every day? God's desire is that every child of Him would experience this fullness that is all sufficient. Do experience the fullness of God we need to know what the fullness of God means. In Col 2:10 the Word says that we are filled with the fullness of God. But what does that mean to you?

When you want to experience this fullness of God, you need to understand the fullness of God. This fullness includes God as the Father, the Son and the Holy Spirit. So many Christians know God as their Saviour or as the Helper but only a few has a relationship with Him as their Father. When we want to know the Lord as our own God we have to have a relationship with Him as a Triune God. God is God the Father, God the Son and God the Holy Spirit.

Many people say they know the Lord, while they are only aware of Him. They know that He exist and they even know that He can do wonders and that He died for their salvation. But still they do not truly know Him. They only know Him for the things they can identify with in their own lives.

I want to explain this by the following example, many people can say that they know their boss. You know his name, what he expects of you at work and how to keep him satisfied at work. But do you really know all his preferences at home, do you know his favourite colour, his favourite food, the name of his parents and all his children. Most of us don't truly know our boss in this way. You interact with him from the understanding you have of him and what you know of him. This is knowing him in just one area of his life, work. But there might be so much more to this person but because you're only involved in the area of work, you only know this area.

So often this is how many Christians know God. They know Him in a certain area of their lives but are not knowing, understanding and trusting Him in all areas of their lives. So many Christians today know God only as God in a specific area ex. healing or provision. While He is God in every area. God is Always and Everything. We need to not only know that God is 'n Triune God, but understand what this mean. When we come to the understanding of Who God as the Father, God as the Son and God as the Spirit is, we will experience Him in so many different ways. God is not only the Creator, He is not only our Saviour and He is not only the Spirit. He is all of this and so much more. He is everything from the Beginning to the End. In order for us to live a life of excellence we need to understand that the God we serve is a God of excellence. In Him is everything we need, we just need to get to know Him in all He is.

When we allow God to be in control in every area of our lives we see how His character and His ways unfold in our lives. And His ways are always higher, better and more prosperous. We need to give over the control to Him and submit to His ways and plans for our lives. He is a good and faithful God and know the plans He has for us. *Jer. 29:11 For I know the thoughts and plans that I have for you, says the Lord, thoughts and plans for welfare and peace, and not for evil, to give you a hope in your final outcome.*

Many people don't know how to have a relationship with God. To experience God in fullness you need to know Him in His fullness. Our God is a Triune God: God the Father, Jesus Christ His Son and the Holy Spirit. To know and experience the fullness of God, we need to know Him as My Lord, Abba Father, Jesus Christ and the Holy Spirit. I hope that as you read through this book you will come to the understanding of who God is for you as an individual, who He wants to be for you and how much He loves you.

Chapter 1

The Lord God

The Word says that God was there from the beginning and that He will be there at the end. Rev 1:8 I am Alpha and Omega, the beginning and the ending, saith the Lord, which is, and which was, and which is to come, the Almighty. He is the same from the beginning until the ends of times.

When you meet someone the first thing you get to know is his or her name. So often we meet our Saviour but never get to know HIS names. When you get an understanding of God's Names, you'll get an understanding of Who He is and Who He wants to be for you. Even from the beginning man realized the importance of God's Name and called Him by His name. *Gen 4:6 And to Seth also a son was born, whom he named Enosh. At that time men began to call (upon God) by the name of the Lord.*

Names are very important in the Bible. The first thing God instructed Adam was to give every creature God created a name. God wanted man to realize and understand the importance and significance of names.

The definition of name is
> **Webster Dictionary—NAME** means:
> * That by which a thing is called; the sound or combination of sounds used to express an idea, or any material substance, quality or act; an

- appellation attached to a thing by customary use, by which it may be vocally distinguished from other things.
* The letters or characters written or engraved, expressing the sounds by which a person or thing is known and distinguished.
* Assumed character of another.

It is clear that from the beginning God wanted man to realize the importance of names. God changed the names of Abraham, Sarah and Saul the moment God changed their situation or their calling. And God instructed people to give specific names ex John the Baptist

- *Gen 17:5 No longer will your name be Abram, but Abraham, for I have made you the father of a number of nations.*
- *Gen 17:15 And God said, As for Sarai, your wife, from now her name will be not Sarai, but Sarah.*

God even said to Moses: "I've called you by your name". Ex 33:12 (KJV) And Moses said unto the LORD, See, thou sayest unto me, Bring up this people: and thou hast not let me know whom thou wilt send with me. Yet thou hast said, *I know thee by name*, and thou hast also found grace in my sight.

God wants us to know the importance of names, so that we would realize the importance of His Names. In different situations God revealed Himself in different names.

The moment we call upon the Name of the Lord, God will answer us. He wants us to have knowledge of Him and the understanding of His names.

Ps. 9:10 And those who have knowledge of your name will put their faith in you; because you, Lord, have ever given your help to those who were waiting for you.

God is still one God but with different characteristics and different attributes.

If we want to experience the fullness of God we need to know and understand all the different ways in which God reveals Himself. One way of getting to know these different attributes of God is to know and understand His different names.

Exo 6:3 And I appeared unto Abraham, unto Isaac, and unto Jacob, by the name of God Almighty (El-Shaddai), but by my name JEHOVAH was I not known to them.

Here God is saying to Moses that He revealed Himself to Abraham, Isaac and Jacob as a supplying and promising God, but He did not reveal Himself to them as Jehovah. Jehovah means God as the One who is existing and the fulfilling God. So here God is saying they only know a part of me, but I am more than that. God is saying to Moses that *I AM*. (Ex 3:14) Here God is telling Moses that He is everything, He is *I AM*.

If you need healing God is saying *I AM* . . . your Healing, if you need provision God is saying *I AM* . . . . your Provision.

In the name of the Lord there is power! Let's look at how God revealed Himself to His people as the Lord God through different names over time.

- Gen 21:33 And *Abraham* planted a grove in Beersheba, and called there on the name of the LORD, the **Everlasting God (Hebr. El Olam)**
- Exo. 33:12. "Yet You said, I know you by name and you have also found favor in My sight.
- Numb. 6:27 And they shall put My name upon the Israelites, and I will bless them.

- *Ps. 20:5 We will triumph at your salvation and victory, and in the name of our God we will set up our banners.*
- *Ps 20:7 Some trust in and boast of chariots and some of horses, but we will trust in and boast of the name of the Lord our God*

Deut 28:10 (ESV) And all the peoples of the earth shall see that you are called by the name of the LORD, and they shall be afraid of you.

God is not just God, He is so much more. I hope that when you study this following list of God's Names you'll realize He is not only God. He is I AM in your every situation. He is your Lord, your Provider, your Healer, your Peace and your Protection and so much more.

The Names of God in the Old Testament

Name	Meaning
Adonai	Lord, Master
El	The Mighty One
Elohim	God, Creator
El Elyon	God Most High
El Olam	The Everlasting God
El Shaddai	Lord God Almighty & All Sufficient One
Jehovah/Yahweh	Lord
Jehovah Jireh	The Lord My Provider
Jehovah Mekoddishkem	The Lord Who Sanctifies
Jehovah Nissi	The Lord is my Banner
Jehovah Raah	The Lord is my Shepherd
Jehovah Rapha	The Lord Who Heals
Jehovah Sabaoth	The Lord of Hosts
Jehovah Shammah	The Lord is There
Jehovah Shalom	The Lord is Peace
Jehovah Tsidkenu	The Lord our Righteousness

When we look at the above mentioned names of God, these are the Names by which God revealed Himself to His people in the Old Testament.

In every situation God's people needed Him, He was able to reveal Himself more and more to them. When Abraham needed provision for an offering, God provided a ram and Abraham called on the Lord as Jehovah Jireh. He got to know God as his Provider.

According to these names of God, we can know that God is:

- **The Lord and Master;**
  The word master (*despotes*) means someone who has absolute ownership and supreme authority (Vine's concise Dictionary). There is nothing that have any power or dominion over our Lord. He is the Master and when we submit ourselves totally unto Him, He will have the supreme authority over us. And as He is a God of goodness, mercy and love, this will be the very things we will see following us when we make Him Lord and Master of our lives. (Ps 23)

- **The Creator of everything**
  Everything came into existence through God and nothing can exist without Him. When we want to live a life of creative miracles and never ending new beginnings we need to submit ourselves to the One who is the Creator. God will always create something good the moment we give to Him what we have. God can take a little when given to Him by us and create with it a lot. A little in the Master's hand, always becomes a lot. Even things that may seem bad, He will turn it around for your good. (Rom 8:28)

- **Almighty**
  Only God is almighty and omnipotent. (Rev. 1:8) Almighty means to be of boundless sufficiency. There is nothing God has not power

over. He is the only One with unlimited might. We know that the enemy is walking around like a roaring lion seeing who he can devours. But God's name is the Almighty! No matter what kind of attack the enemy launch against you, if you are calling on the Name of the Lord, He is Almighty. He is the One who has all power and boundless sufficiency to deal with the enemy. No weapon formed against you as His child can prosper. (Is. 54:11)

- **All Sufficient**
  Our God is everything we need. He is Life, He gives Life and He wants to be in control of our lives. The moment we surrender ourselves to Him and we learn to depend on Him for our every need, decision and actions, we will see His glory manifesting in our lives.

- **Sanctifier**
  Is 1:18 "Come now, let us reason together, says the LORD: though your sins are like scarlet, they shall be as white as snow; though they are red like crimson, they shall become like wool. We can't forgive our own sins, we can't redeem ourselves we need our Saviour to do it for us. We are so blessed to have a God who says no matter how great our sins are, He is faithful and just to forgive us our sins. Many people are still trapped in their old ways and sins in their past. When God forgives you, He sanctifies you completely! You become totally new! Don't wait another day—if there is any sin that you need to repent of, to it right now.

The Word says if we will confess then God will forgive us.
1John 1:9 If we confess our sins, he is faithful and just to forgive us *our* sins, and to cleanse us from all unrighteousness.
If you need to confess any sin pray the following prayer:
Dear Lord Jesus I confess that I have sinned, (name the sin that you are repenting off) I ask You to forgive me and cleanse me with Your

blood. Please help me not to commit these same sins again. I thank you in the Name of Jesus Christ. Amen

Now you are cleansed, pure as snow. If you need to forgive someone or yourself. Speak that forgiveness right now, and see how God will make a way for you where there seems no way.

- **Your Banner**

   When the bible speak of God as our Banner it refers to Him as being our protection and our aid. His presence is surrounding us like a banner. Therefore when we call upon God as our Banner we see how He is protecting us, and how He is intervening on our behalf. A banner is the first thing you see when you approach a place that is covered by a banner. The same it will be with you. When God is your Banner, it will be the first thing the enemy sees when he tries to attack you. As long as you confess God as Jehovah Nissi the enemy has no right to attack you. He has been defeated by our Lord Jesus!

- **Your Provision**

   Do you still depend on your own strength, your salary or your spouse to provide for you? Then it will always be changing. This world and it's systems are always changing and nothing is for certain. But when we start to see God as Jehovah Jireh, and He become our Provider we will always have more than enough. God is not a God of enough, He is a God of abundance! The problem is that there is a very little percentage of the Lord's children that is 100% dependant on Him for their provision. Most Christians believe that God can provide for them, but trust in themselves to make it happen. In who is your trust? Is it in Jehovah Jireh and only in Him you trust for your provision? There is more than 2000 scriptures of God's blessing and provision. Stand on His Word and you will never experience lack in your life.

- **Your Healing**
  Healing is not something God would consider, God is Healing! Jesus went about and healed ALL who were sick. When one speak about God healing people it is like opening a can of worms. People don't have the faith that God is still healing His people today. The problem is not that God changed, the problem lies with us. We don't have the faith to receive the healing God wants to give every child of Him.
  Jesus commanded the disciples to go and heal the sick. Mat 10:1 And he called to him his twelve disciples and gave them authority over unclean spirits, to cast them out, and to heal every disease and every affliction.

  God didn't change His mind, nor did His character change. He is still the same God, Jehovah Rapha, our Healer. He wants you to be healthy and has given you the authority to pray for the sick. Just have faith in Him as the Healer and let Him do the healing.

  James 5:14 & 15 Is anyone among you sick? Let him call for the elders of the church, and let them pray over him, anointing him with oil in the name of the Lord. And the prayer of faith will save the one who is sick, and the Lord will raise him up. And if he has committed sins, he will be forgiven.

- **Your Peace**
  When we confess God as our Lord and Peace the word used is Jehovah Shalom. A very dear friend of mine's mother, Eileen de Jager spend years on researching the word Shalom. This is how she has defined it:

> ### What the word SHALOM means:
>
> *The word SHALOM, which is usually translated* **Peace**,
> *means much more than simply peace.*
> *It means: "The peace from the Almighty that destroys the force that brings chaos into our life!"*
> *And it also means:*
> ***To be complete***
> ***Nothing missing,***
> ***Nothing broken.***
> ***To be happy and secure***
> *To be in harmonious unity with God and fellowman*
> *To be safe and satisfied, unharmed and unhurt.*
> *To be content, faithful, whole and balanced.*
> *To experience satisfaction with life and the absence of all strife, As well as prosperity, loyalty, justice, mercy and peace.*
> *And according to the Amplified Bible:*
> ***"Tranquility of heart and life continually!"***
> *WHAT A BEAUTIFUL, MEANINGFUL WORD SHALOM IS!*

This is such a beautiful definition of the word peace but more it is a perfect description of the God we serve. The moment we call upon Him as Jehovah Shalom we experience completeness, fulfilment, healing, security, love, joy and everything we need! Dare to call on God as Jehovah Shalom, you will see how your life and heart become continually tranquil.

- **Your Hosts**

  This is the name that David used as he challenged Goliath: "You come against me with sword and spear and javelin," David said, "but I come to you in the name of Jehovah of Hosts [1 Sam. 17:45, Recovery version]" So often you may be facing a giant in your life. Don't try to fight the difficult situations in your own strength. Call on the name that has been given to you as child of God—Jehovah Sabaoth! He has defeated Goliath, He will defeat your giants too. Have faith to trust Him with the giants in your live.

- **Always There**
We live in a world where nothing is certain. The fact that you are married, have children, have a job or a house. All these can change and then you could no longer be married. If your boss decides to hire someone else, you could be jobless. As children of God we have something that the world can never give us. Something that is always there and never changing. This is our Lord, Jehovah Shamah! God is always there for us, He will never leave us nor forsake us. (Heb 13:5, Jos 1:5) No matter what you go through, where you are—call upon the Lord as Jehovah Shamah and believe that He is there for you. People will disappoint us, people will let us down, but the Lord will never let His people be put to shame. (Rom 10:11)

- **Your Shepherd**
As children we learn Ps 23 and we can say it like a poem. But do we really have faith in the Lord as our Shepherd. (John 10:11)
What is a Shepherd? A shepherd is not only feeding his flock, he is also protecting them. A shepherd is willing to spend hours to care for his flock. He will carry the ones that's hurt and will look for the lost. The important thing is though if you want the Lord to be your Shepherd you need to become part of the flock. Have you given your life to the Lord Jesus as Your Saviour. We cannot be saved because we do good deeds or because our family are saved. You need to give your life to the Lord. If you haven't done this ever before, only attending church or being part of a group believers,

will not safe you. If you need to give your life to the Lord, pray this prayer:

Lord Jesus, I confess today that I am a sinner. I want to make You my Saviour. I believe with my heart and confess with my mouth that You died for me on the cross. That you were buried and on the third day you rose again. I believe that You are the Son of God and that You are sitting at the right hand of the Father. I ask that You forgive me my sins and make me Your child. In Jesus Name. Amen.

- **Your Righteousness**
The Lord Jesus is our Righteousness. Because of the complete work of Jesus Christ on the cross, we are righteous. We are in right standing with God and has the right to freely enter God's presence. Before Jesus died on the cross the Lord met with His people in the tabernacle. In the Holy of Holies the Lord's presence were manifested and only the High Priest had entrance once a year. Once Jesus died on the cross the veil was torn and now we as children of God has the right to seek God's presence everyday.

Rom 5:17 For if, because of one man's trespass, death reigned through that one man, much more will those who receive the abundance of grace and the free gift of righteousness reign in life through the one man Jesus Christ.

Righteousness is a free gift, you can't earn it, we don't deserve it but receive it as a free gift when we accept Jesus Christ as our Saviour. Our God is not interest in how good we are, or what we can give or do for Him, but what He did for us. We just need to accept this gift and then we become righteous!

This is just a few names by which the Israelites called upon the Lord and already it covers everything we need for a life of victory and abundance.

If you think about your own life, is there any situation that you can think about, that God cannot change, intervene or resolve by calling on the Name of the Lord. God is not only the Almighty, All Sufficient, and Omni-present God. He is also our Protection, our Peace, He is always There and He is our Righteousness.

There is still so much more to the names of God. God is continually revealing Himself to His children in different names. There is more than 365 names of God. Take the time and study the names of God so that they may become more than just knowledge to you. The moment you understand the power that there is on calling on the Name that is above every Name, the Name that is always the same, you will see how the Lord will change your circumstances.

The Lord is still I Am . . . even for you!

This is a list compiled an unknown author which include scriptures of Who God is.

Here is a list of the Names of God in the Old and New Testament

Advocate—1 John 2:1
Almighty—Revelation 1:8
Alpha—Revelation 1:8
Amen—Revelation 3:14
Angel of the Lord—Genesis 16:7
Anointed One—Psalm 2:2
Apostle—Hebrews 3:1
Author and Perfecter of our Faith—Hebrews 12:2
Beginning—Revelation 21:6
Bishop of Souls—1 Peter 2:25
Branch—Zechariah 3:8
Bread of Life—John 6:35,48

Bridegroom—Matthew 9:15
Carpenter—Mark 6:3
Chief Shepherd—1 Peter 5:4
The Christ—Matthew 1:16
Comforter—Jeremiah 8:18
Consolation of Israel—Luke 2:25
Cornerstone—Ephesians 2:20
Dayspring—Luke 1:78
Day Star—2 Peter 1:19
Deliverer—Romans 11:26
Desire of Nations—Haggai 2:7
Emmanuel—Matthew 1:23
End—Revelation 21:6
Everlasting Father—Isaiah 9:6
Faithful and True Witness—Revelation 3:14
First Fruits—1 Corinthians 15:23
Foundation—Isaiah 28:16
Fountain—Zechariah 13:1
Friend of Sinners—Matthew 11:19
Gate for the Sheep—John 10:7
Gift of God—2 Corinthians 9:15
God—John 1:1
Glory of God—Isaiah 60:1
Good Shepherd—John 10:11
Governor—Matthew 2:6
Great Shepherd—Hebrews 13:20
Guide—Psalm 48:14
Head of the Church—Colossians 1:18
High Priest—Hebrews 3:1
Holy One of Israel—Isaiah 41:14
Horn of Salvation—Luke 1:69
I Am—Exodus 3:14
Jehovah—Psalm 83:18

The Fullness of God

Jesus—Matthew 1:21
King of Israel—Matthew 27:42
King of Kings—1 Timothy 6:15; Revelation 19:16
Lamb of God—John 1:29
Last Adam—1 Corinthians 15:45
Life—John 11:25
Light of the World—John 8:12; John 9:5
Lion of the Tribe of Judah—Revelation 5:5
Lord of Lords—1 Timothy 6:15; Revelation 19:16
Master—Matthew 23:8
Mediator—1 Timothy 2:5
Messiah—John 1:41
Mighty God—Isaiah 9:6
Morning Star—Revelation 22:16
Nazarene—Matthew 2:23
Omega—Revelation 1:8
Passover Lamb—1 Corinthians 5:7
Physician—Matthew 9:12
Potentate—1 Timothy 6:15
Priest—Hebrews 4:15
Prince of Peace—Isaiah 9:6
Prophet—Acts 3:22
Propitiation—I John 2:2
Purifier—Malachi 3:3
Rabbi—John 1:49
Ransom—1 Timothy 2:6
Redeemer—Isaiah 41:14
Refiner—Malachi 3:2
Refuge—Isaiah 25:4
Resurrection—John 11:25
Righteousness—Jeremiah 23:6
Rock—Deuteronomy 32:4
Root of David—Revelation 22:16

Rose of Sharon—Song of Solomon 2:1
Ruler of God's Creation—Revelation 3:14
Sacrifice—Ephesians 5:2
Savior—2 Samuel 22:47; Luke 1:47
Second Adam—1 Corinthians 15:47
Seed of *Abraham*—Galatians 3:16
Seed of David—2 Timothy 2:8
Seed of the Woman—Genesis 3:15
Servant—Isaiah 42:1
Shepherd—1 Peter 2:25
Shiloh—Genesis 49:10
Son of David—Matthew 15:22
Son of God—Luke 1:35
Son of Man—Matthew 18:11
Son of Mary—Mark 6:3
Son of the Most High—Luke 1:32
Stone—Isaiah 28:16
Sun of Righteousness—Malachi 4:2
Teacher—Matthew 26:18
Truth—John 14:6
Way—John 14:6
Wonderful Counselor—Isaiah 9:6
Word—John 1:1
Vine—John 15:1

Chapter 2

The Lord, Jesus Christ

John 1:16 For out of His fullness (abundance) we have all received (all had a share and we were all supplied with) one grace after another and spiritual blessing upon spiritual blessing and even favor upon favor and gift (heaped) upon gift.

In chapter 1 we spoke about God as a Triune God. We've talked about God's Names and the importance of calling on His name. As we mentioned God is a Triune God, God the Father, the Son and the Holy Spirit.

In this chapter we'll focus on Jesus Christ as the Word of God. The first time the word Jesus is written is in Matthew 1:1, the New Testament. This doesn't mean that Jesus was not part of the Old Testament. Through the whole Old Testament there is a proto type of Jesus revealed to us. As we've seen Jesus was there from the very beginning and He will be coming for His Bride at the end.

In the beginning was the Word, and the Word was with God, and the Word was God. He was in the beginning with God. All things were made through him, and without him was not any thing made that was made. (John 1:1-3).

Through Jesus we have the authority to become children of God and to call upon His name. We've already discussed the importance of God's names. Adding on to this now we have the right to call Him Father. Our God is the only God that although He is Almighty and Powerful, He also want to have a relationship with us as His children. Therefore we can get to know Him also as Father (Chapter 4)

The first prophecy of Jesus was spoken by God in Genesis 3:15. From Genesis 3 God was planning the birth of His Son as the Seed that will come and bruise the head of the enemy. It was through sin that evil entered into the world and since then an offering was needed for the forgiveness of sin. Through out the Old Testament we read how God's people made offerings for forgiveness. With the birth of Jesus Christ, God fulfilled the prophecy of the Seed that will bruise the head of the enemy.

The offerings of the Old Testament had to be done every year, because there was no one without sin to bring a perfect offering. Therefore the priest had to bring these offering on behalf of the people. We see that the priest had to sprinkle the blood seven times. **Lev 4:6** *And the priest is to put his finger in the blood, shaking drops of it before the Lord seven times, in front of the veil of the holy place.*

Lev 16:19 *Shaking drops of the blood from his finger on it seven times to make it holy and clean from whatever is unclean among the children of Israel.*

Seven is the number of completion and perfection. God created the earth in seven days and the blood had to be sprinkled seven times.

When Jesus was crucified, He became the perfect sacrifice for the forgiveness of the sin of the world. **Heb 10:12** *But when Jesus had made one offering for sins for ever, he took his place at the right hand of God;*

Jesus is the One Offering for our sins that was perfect and because He also shed His blood seven times, the offering is complete. He shed His blood for us, so that we can be saved forever and through that the enemy has no right to accuse us. Before Jesus died Satan had access to God but after Jesus was crucified Satan has no right to bring any charge against God's children. Jesus is sitting at the right hand of the Father as our Perfect Sacrifice, once and for all.

Just as it was required to sprinkle seven drops of blood as a sacrifice so Jesus shed His blood seven times for you and me.

Let's look at how His sacrifice was the complete and perfect sacrifice so that we can live a fulfilling, abundant life. **Hebrew 9:11-15**

The seven blood shedding of Jesus Christ as the perfect sacrifice

(i) The blood drops in the garden of Gethsemane

***Luke 22:44** And being in an agony he prayed more earnestly: and his sweat was as it were great drops of blood falling down to the ground.*

The first ever blood sacrifice was in a garden, the garden of Eden where Satan tempted the first Adam. Jesus as the second Adam, once again in a garden, shed the first drop of blood to be the perfect and final sacrifice for us.

The fall of mankind started in a garden, and in the garden of Gethsemane the restoration of mankind started. Before Jesus started praying He once again warned the disciples to pray that they do not enter in temptation. In the garden of Eden through temptation Satan captured mankind and ever since mankind didn't have freedom to reign as God intended them to. Jesus too was captured in the garden. Only this time to restore the freedom God intended for His children. Those who the Son sets free is free indeed. Jesus was captured so that you can live a life of freedom and liberty.

The scripture says that Jesus sweat while praying in the garden. In the beginning when man fell for Satan' lie, God said in the sweat of your face you will earn your bread. (Gen 3:19) This sin of man brought the curse of having to sweat to earn anything. When Jesus sweat and the first blood offering was shed, this curse was broken. Jesus said: *"the thief does not come except to steal and kill and destroy; I came so that you may have life and may have it abundantly." (John 10:10)*

Proverbs. 10:22 The blessing of the Lord makes one rich, and He adds no sorrow with it

Ps 127:2 It is in vain that you rise up early and go late to rest, eating the bread of anxious toil; for he gives to his beloved sleep.

Jesus broke the curse that was on finances and brought us the freedom to be blessed according to His ways. Abundant living is now not only for those who work 20 hours per day, but for every child of God who is living according to His Word and walking in His ways.

(ii) The stripes on His back for our healing

Luk 22:63 *The men who were guarding Jesus made fun of him and beat him.*

Isa 53:5 *But He was wounded for our transgressions, He was bruised for our iniquities. The chastisement for our peace was upon Him, and by His* ***stripes we are healed.***

Because Jesus was beaten and crushed we were healed. (1Pet 2:24) Jesus took all sickness and every disease upon Him, we are healed not by what we do right but because He took it upon Himself to be beaten for our iniquities. Sickness is part of the world we live in but it need not be part of your life. We are in the world but we are not from this world. The moment you accept Jesus Christ as your Saviour, you are not from this world any longer. You are adopted into the kingdom of God. In God's kingdom there is no sickness. To live a life without any sickness is not only a possibility for God's children, it is a principal the Word of God states.

Whatever sickness you may have, have faith that God wants to heal you. As we saw in the previous chapter God is Jehovah Jireh and therefore calling on His name and being His child you can live a healthy life. The choice is yours to accept it through faith.

(iii) Jesus bled in His face

Isaiah 50:6 *"I gave my back to the smiters, and my cheeks to them that plucked off the hair; I hid not my face from shame and spitting"*

Jesus bled in His face, and He took the shame upon Him, so that you and I do not have to be ashamed. God promise us that His people will never be put to shame. ***Rom 10:11*** For the Scripture says, "Whoever believes on Him will not be put to shame".

Now that Jesus took all the guilt and shame on Himself even though He did not deserve any of this, we don't have to struggle with feelings of guilt and condemnation. There is therefore now no condemnation to those who are in Christ Jesus. (Rom 8:1) Shame and guilt are the two things that keep so many people from serving God fully. It is only the enemy that reminds us of our past and that brings feelings of guilt and shame. We serve a God that was willing to take it all upon Himself so that you can have it all. Through Jesus we are freed from the law of sin and death. As a child of God the power that sin had over man was broken.

(iv) The crown of thorns—blood running down His face

John 19:2 *and the soldiers platted a crown of thorns, and put it on His head,* When they put the crown of thorns on Jesus' head He bled so that we can be renewed. Our thoughts and thinking and our mind are cleansed by the blood of Jesus. Now we should be renewed by our mind—daily.

Rom 12:2 *And do not be conform to this world, but be transformed by the renewing of your mind, that you may prove what is that good and acceptable and perfect will of God.*

A crown is a symbol of royalty and victory. In the beginning God gave man the authority to reign over the earth. Man was the ruler and was crowned with honor and glory. When satan tempted man, wickedness started to reign and man ruled in a way God didn't approve off. When Jesus was crowned, he took back the crown and authority so that we can once again rule on earth.

Rev 1:6 *And have made us kings and priests unto God and his Father; to him be glory and dominion for ever and ever. Amen.*

We are more than conquerors and with Jesus we can do anything. He gave us all the power and authority we need to accomplish that what He sends us to do. (Rom 8:37)

(v) His hands bled for us

When they nailed Jesus's hands to the cross, His blood was shed for the work of our hands so that we can prosper and that everything we do can be successful. ***Deut 28:8*** *the Lord will command the blessing on you in your storehouses and in all to which you set your hand,*

God wants you to be blessed and to be prosperous. He wants to give you the desires of your heart. (Ps 37:4) Jesus blood was shed so that we may enter into His presence with clean hands. In the Old Testament the priest had to wash their hands every time they enter into the tabernacle. (Ex 30:19) The Word explains that we are washed by the Blood of the Lamb and through God's Word. The Blood of the Lamb is the blood of Jesus and He also is the Word (John 1). Therefore if we accept Jesus as our Saviour and confess our sin, we don't have to wash our hands and bring a offering for the remission of our sins. Jesus's hands bled so that we may enter the presence of God with boldness.

(vi) Jesus's feet bled for us

When they nailed Jesus's feet to the cross He shed His blood as a sacrifice to give us authority back. Now we have the authority to trample on serpents and scorpions (Luk 10:19). Now, where your feet will step, believe that God will be with you. Believe that as for Joshua, He will increase your territory.

Jos. 1:3 Every place that the sole of your foot will tread upon I have given you,

As said God gave man dominion over the earth, but through sin, satan took control of the earth. Jesus bled so that this dominion could be restored. We have to take up the authority given to us by Jesus Christ as the perfect sacrifice. *Psalm 8:6 You have given him dominion over the works of Your hands; You have put all things under his feet,*

Jesus is the Rock and now our feet are set upon Him, therefore if we trust in Him, we will not slip nor fall. He will give His angels charge over us, they protect us and will keep us from getting hurt. (Psalm 91)

When Jesus shed His blood, the enemy was placed under His feet and has no dominion over Him since. Therefore if we are in Christ Jesus we have authority over the enemy and can demand Him to stay under our feet.

(vii) The spear in His side

John 19:34 *But one of the soldiers pierced His side with a spear, and immediately blood and water came out.*

Eve was formed from a rib from Adam side. Jesus was the second Adam. And when the spear pierced Him in His side, we received eternal life, once again from the side of the perfect Adam.

1Co 15:45 *For the scripture says, "The first man, Adam, was created a living being"; but the last Adam is the life-giving Spirit.*

Only now we are not living according to the dictates of the flesh but according to the dictates of the Spirit. We need to be led by the Holy Spirit in our daily living.

Through the complete and perfect sacrifice Jesus Christ on the cross:

- we are freed from every curse (Gal 3:13);
- we have liberty and freedom (Luke 4:18)
- we have the blessing of provision (Phil 4:19)
- We are healed (1 Pet 2:24)
- We are more than conquerors (Rom 8:37)
- We live without condemnation, shame and guilt (Rom 8:1)
- We will receive the crown of glory (1 Pet 5:4)
- We can prosper (John 10:10)
- we have authority (Luk 10:19)
- we have dominion (Rev. 1:6)
- we have a new life (Rom 6:4)

In summary we can thus say that because of the perfect and complete Sacrifice we are now children of the Lord and therefore we can cry out Abba Father! (Rom 8:14 & 15). So because the Word of God, Jesus Christ became flesh, lived among men and then was crucified, we can now have a relationship with the Lord as our Abba Father.

Chapter 3

The Lord our Father

In the previous chapter we read how the Lord, Jesus Christ is the Son of God. Because of the complete work Jesus has done, we are now called children of God. We are not only worshippers of God, when we accepts Jesus as our personal Saviour we become sons and daughters of the Lord. **2Co 6:18** *and I will be a father to you, and you shall be sons and daughters to me, says the Lord Almighty."* We have the right to call on the Lord, not only as the Lord and His Name but as our Father.

This is what is making our God so awesome. He is not only God, Almighty and Sovereign, He is longing for an intimate relationship with His followers.

God is not interested in how good we can worship Him, He is interested in us having a father-child relationship with Him.

When we talk about the Lord often people could relate to God as Jesus and acknowledge the Holy Spirit. But so often we find that it is difficult to identify with the Lord as Abba Father. Even in the Word we read how Jesus needed to teach the people about the Lord as Father. Only then the apostles and the people could address the Lord as Father. Isa 9:6 For to us a child is born, to us a son is given; and the government shall be upon his shoulder, and his name shall be called Wonderful Counselor, Mighty God, *Everlasting Father*, Prince of Peace.

In the Old Testament we don't read that the people knew God as their Father. They only knew God as the Lord. We've discussed in the previous chapter how God revealed His Glory and His majesty in different ways at different times to His people. His Names were known and they called upon the Lord as His Name. I could only find a few scriptures in the Old Testament where the Lord is described as Father.

Deut 32:6 Do you thus repay the LORD, you foolish and senseless people? Is not He your Father, who created you, who made you and established you?

Mal 2:10 Have we not all one Father? hath not one God created us? why do we deal treacherously every man against his brother, by profaning the covenant of our fathers?

It is clear that the reality of God as the Father was not something all the Israelites understood. Many of them only believed in God as the Lord.

They feared God and worship Him as Lord God the Almighty, Self Existing and Eternal God.

Through the birth of Jesus Christ as the Son of God, people started to realize that God is not only their Lord, but He is also their Father. **Rom 8:15** *For you have not received the spirit of bondage again to fear; but you have received the Spirit of adoption, whereby we cry, Abba, Father.* This is a very important part of our relationship with God that is so often the area in which people don't know God. As with the Israelites people can believe in God and in all He can do, but cannot trust in Him like a child trust his father.

The fact that God is not only our Lord but also our Father is the very thing that makes our believe in God not a religion but so much more. We can have a relationship with our God not only for what He wants of us but with whom we are created to be.

Let's look at the role of a father in the family. A father is the one who is protecting his family, he is the one taking care of their daily needs and making sure his family is safe and secure. A father has the right to discipline his children and he has the privilege of the children bearing his name. A father does not only discipline his children but he also guides them. When we read proverbs there are many principal for a father-child relationship.

The Lord wants to be more than just Provider, Healer and Protector to us. He wants to be your Abba Father. To become a child of God is something we cannot earn by doing good. It is only through Jesus Christ that we can become sons and daughters of the Lord (John 14:6). As soon as you have accepted Jesus Christ as your personal Saviour you become a child in God's Kingdom.

Being a child gives you a right, not only certain privileges. You have a right to stand on the statements made in the New Testament. A testament become active the moment someone pass away. When Jesus died on the cross for us as the perfect Sacrifice, the New Testament became valid.

We are not only servants and worshipers of the Lord we are now children and therefore we have the right to claim the rights that are set out for us in the Word.

Gal 4:6 And because you are sons, God have sent forth the Spirit of his Son into your hearts, crying, Abba, Father!

When one is a child there is a dependency on your father. As a child of The Father we should be dependant only on Him. We can stand upon the Word and proclaim that what is written is yes and amen. When we need any guidance we should consult our Father. He will give us the right guidance to bless us and keep us safe. (Ps 31:3, Isa 58:11)

A relationship with the Lord as Father is not a religion. Religion ask of us to perform and to be good. Our Father ask only for us to love Him with our whole heart, mind and soul. The more we love Him, the more we will want to be like Him. God as the Father is interested in each one of His children and has a unique calling and gifting for every one. He is not interested in forming a group of people that is all the same because they have to be. Our Father is not full of expectancy of His children, but has a great expectancy for us. He's plans and thoughts are only to give us hope and a future, to keep us and bless us. (Jer. 29:11)

The privileges in the New Testament includes:

- Being cared for
- Being looked after
- being protected
- being blessed
- being loved
- being healthy
- being part of a family
- being prosperous
- being powerful
- being fruitful
- being chosen
- being royalty
- being able

Chapter 4

Holy Spirit

John 14:26 But the Comforter (Counselor, Helper, Intercessor, Advocate, Strenghtener, Standby) the Holy Spirit, Whom the Father will send in My Name (in My place, to represent Me and act on My behalf), He will teach you all things. And He will cause you to recall (will remind you of, bring to your remembrance), everything I have told you. (Amplified)

Joh 20:22 And when he had said this, breathing on them, he said to them, Let the Holy Spirit come on you:

Who is the Holy Spirit God?

Gen 1:2 The earth was without form and void, and darkness was over the face of the deep. And the Spirit of God was hovering over the face of the waters.

The Spirit of God was there from the beginning. God is the same from the beginning and will be the same for eternity. God doesn't change. The Spirit of God is omnipresent and we can't escape the Spirit of God. *(Ps 139:7 Where may I go from your spirit? how may I go in flight from you?)*

The Holy Spirit is the third person of the Triune God. We've talked about God the Father, Jesus Christ the Son and now we'll talk about the third entity the Spirit of God. Remember although God is Three He also still is One. One God in three persons is the mystery of the divine Trinity.

The Spirit where thus there when God created the earth and man and the Holy Spirit is here with us today. God says that we only need the Holy Spirit to teach us. *1John 2:27 But as for you, Christ has poured out his Spirit on you. As long as his Spirit remains in you, you do not need anyone to teach you. For his Spirit teaches you about everything, and what He teaches is true, not false. Obey the Spirit's teaching, then, and remain in union with Christ.*

For the Holy Spirit to teach you, you need to know who the Spirit is. The Word says that at the end times there will be many false spirits and that we need to test the spirits whether it is the Holy Spirit.

1John 4:1 Beloved, do not believe every spirit, but test the spirits to see whether they are from God, for many false prophets have gone out into the world.

Rev 3:1 "And to the angel of the church in Sardis write: 'The words of him who has the <u>seven</u> <u>spirits</u> <u>of</u> <u>God</u> and the seven stars.'"I know your works. You have the reputation of being alive, but you are dead.

The Holy Spirit is one but has seven important manifestations. These seven Spirits are continually before the throne of God. (Rev 4:5)

Isa 11:2 And the Spirit of the LORD shall rest upon him, the Spirit of wisdom and understanding, the Spirit of counsel and might, the Spirit of knowledge and the fear of the LORD.

(1) Spirit of the Lord
(2) Spirit of wisdom
(3) Spirit of understanding

(4) Spirit of counsel
(5) Spirit of might
(6) Spirit of knowledge
(7) Spirit of fear of the Lord

You'll only be able to discern between the spirits if you know who the Holy Spirit is. The Word teaches us who the Spirit of God is. Let's look at some of the attributes of the Holy Spirit:

- The Spirit of God was at work in the original act of creation (Genesis 1:2);
- He continually sustains the universe (Job 34:14-15); He is everywhere dynamically present (Ps. 139:7-8);
- and through His power the conception of the Son of God in the womb of the Virgin Mary occurred (Luke 1:35).
- The Holy Spirit also brings about conviction of sin and by Him the new birth takes place (John 3:6 and 16:8);
- He indwells all true believers (Romans 8:4); He is the agent of ongoing sanctification (2 Cor. 3:18);
- and some day in the Resurrection, He will give life to our mortal bodies (Rom. 8:11).

It is evident that the Holy Spirit is the Person in the divine Trinity who is powerfully at work in relation to all that God has made.

He gives life: *Mat 1:18 Now the birth of Jesus Christ was in this way: when his mother Mary was going to be married to Joseph, before they came together the discovery was made that she was with child by the Holy Spirit.*

Job 33:4 *The spirit of God has made me, and the breath of the Ruler of all gives me life.*

Joh 6:63 *The spirit is the life giver; the flesh is of no value: the words which I have said to you are spirit and they are life.*

He is gentle and soft:

Mat 3:16 And Jesus, having been given baptism, straight away went up from the water; and, the heavens opening, he saw the Spirit of God coming down on him as a dove;

He gives wisdom and insight:

Gen 41:38 Then Pharaoh said to his servants, Where may we get such a man as this, a man in whom is the spirit of God?

Gen 41:39 And Pharaoh said to Joseph, Seeing that God has made all this clear to you, there is no other man of such wisdom and good sense as you:

Deut 34:9 And Joshua, the son of Nun, was full of the spirit of wisdom; for Moses had put his hands on him: and the children of Israel gave ear to him, and did as the Lord had given orders to Moses.

Joel 2:28 And after that, it will come about, says the Lord, that I will send my spirit on all flesh; and your sons and your daughters will be prophets, your old men will have dreams, your young men will see visions:

He gives talents & creativity:

Exo 28:3 Give orders to all the wise-hearted workmen, whom I have made full of the spirit of wisdom, to make robes for Aaron, so that he may be made holy as my priest.

Exo 31:3 And I have given him the spirit of God and made him wise and full of knowledge and expert in every sort of handwork,

Exo 35:31 And he has made him full of the spirit of God, in all wisdom and knowledge and art of every sort;

Dan 5:12 Because a most special spirit, and knowledge and reason and the power of reading dreams and unfolding dark sayings and answering hard questions, were seen to be in him, even in Daniel

He gives strength and power:

Jdg 14:6 And the spirit of the Lord came on him with power, and, unarmed as he was, pulling the lion in two as one might do to a young goat, he put him to death; but he said nothing to his father

1Sam 10:6 And the spirit of the Lord will come on you with power, and you will be acting like a prophet with them, and will be changed into another man.

1Sam 16:13 Then Samuel took the bottle of oil, and put the oil on him there among his brothers: and from that day the spirit of the Lord came on David with power.

Act 1:8 But you will have power, when the Holy Spirit has come on you; and you will be my witnesses in Jerusalem and all Judaea

Act 2:4 And they were all full of the Holy Spirit, and were talking in different languages, as the Spirit gave them power.

He brings freedom:

Judges 15:14 And when he came to Lehi, the Philistines came out, meeting him with loud cries; then the spirit of the Lord came rushing on him, and the cords on his arms became like grass which has been burned with fire, and the bands came falling off his hands.

Luke 1:67 And his father, Zacharias, was full of the Holy Spirit, and with the voice of a prophet said these words:

Luke 1:68 Praise be to the Lord, the God of Israel, for he has come to his people and made them free,

He gives knowledge:

Luke 2:26 And he had knowledge, through the Holy Spirit, that he

John 14:17 Even the Spirit of true knowledge. That Spirit the world is not able to take to its heart because it sees him not and has no knowledge of him: but you have knowledge of him, because he is ever with you and will be in you.

John 16:13 However, when he, the Spirit of true knowledge, has come, he will be your guide into all true knowledge

He gives guidance:

Ps 143:10 Give me teaching so that I may do your pleasure; for you are my God: let your good Spirit be my guide into the land of righteousness.

Ezek 36:27 And I will put my spirit in you, causing you to be guided by my rules, and you will keep my orders and do them.

Luk 12:12 For the Holy Spirit will make clear to you in that very hour what to say.

New life:

Joh 3:6 That which has birth from the flesh is flesh, and that which has birth from the Spirit is spirit.

Gives us sonship:

John 4:24 God is Spirit: then let his worshippers give him worship in the true way of the spirit.

He brings healing & good news:

Isa 61:1 The spirit of the Lord is on me, because I am marked out by him to give good news to the poor; he has sent me to make the broken-hearted well, to say that the prisoners will be made free, and that those in chains will see the light again;

Luke 4:18 The Spirit of the Lord is on me, because I am marked out by him to give good news to the poor; he has sent me to make well those who are broken-hearted; to say that the prisoners will be let go, and the blind will see, and to make the wounded free from their chains,

He brings joy:

Luke 10:21 *In that same hour he was full of joy in the Holy Spirit and said, I give praise to you, O Father, Lord of heaven and earth, because you have kept these things secret from the wise and the men of learning, and have made them clear to little children: for so, O Father, it was pleasing in your eyes.*

He brings peace and cancel fear:

Hag 2:5 *The agreement which I made with you when you came out of Egypt, and my spirit, are with you still; have no fear.*

He teach you and give you words:

Mat 10:20 *Because it is not you who say the words, but the Spirit of your Father in you.*

John 14:26 *But the Helper, the Holy Spirit, whom the Father will send in my name, will be your teacher in all things and will put you in mind of everything I have said to you.*

He equips us to be His servant:

Matt 12:18 *See my servant, the man of my selection, my loved one in whom my soul is well pleased: I will put my Spirit on him, and he will make my decision clear to the Gentiles.*

He is always ready:

Mark 14:38 Keep watch with prayer, so that you may not be put to the test; the spirit truly is ready, but the flesh is feeble.

When we look at all these attributes of the Holy Spirit, we can all agree that we need the Holy Spirit in our daily living. Jesus said that He is going away but that He will send us the Helper, Comforter, Strength. (John 14)

Jesus even said to His disciples not to go out from Jerusalem before they received the Holy Spirit (Acts 1:4 & 8) Jesus said the Holy Spirit will give them power to be His witnesses. This means that we shouldn't do things out of our own strength. A good idea, is not always a Godly idea. We need to wait upon the Holy Spirit that will give us the power to do the Godly thing.

But how do I receive the Spirit?

The Holy Spirit is given by our Heavenly Father. The Spirit is not something we can earn. God give the Holy Spirit as a gift to His children. Therefore you first have to accept Jesus Christ as your Saviour, then you are a child of God and you will receive the gift of the Holy Spirit. God always work with a willing heart. God is waiting for us to ask of Him, and when we ask we will receive. **Luke 11:13** *If you then, who are evil, know how to give good gifts to your children, how much more will the heavenly Father give the Holy Spirit to those who ask him!"*

John explained to the people that it is only Jesus that could baptizes with the Holy Spirit. The Holy Spirit cannot operate when Jesus is not the Lord of your life. As soon as you accept Jesus as you Saviour, the Holy Spirit will fill you.

John 1:33 I myself did not know him, but he who sent me to baptize with water said to me, 'He on whom you see the Spirit descend and remain, this is he who baptizes with the Holy Spirit.'

Being baptize with the Spirit is strange to many people. What does it mean to be baptized with the Spirit is the question many people asks?

Baptism with the Holy Spirit is a distinctive experience referred to in all the gospels and in the Book of Acts. According to Mark 1:8 John the Baptist said, "I baptized you with water; but He will baptize you with the Holy Spirit." In Acts 1:5, Jesus Himself declared, "John baptized with water, but you shall be baptized with the Holy Spirit not many days from now." Accordingly, on the Day of Pentecost the promise of John and Jesus was fulfilled when believing disciples in Jerusalem "were all filled with the Holy Spirit and began to speak with other tongues, as the Spirit was giving them utterance" (Acts 2:4).

This baptism with the Spirit did not end with the Day of Pentecost. Years later in Caesarea there was an outpouring of the Holy Spirit on believing Gentiles—"The gift of the Holy Spirit had been poured out upon the Gentiles also . . . speaking in tongues and exalting God" (Acts 10:45-46). About this event Peter later declared, "I remembered the word of the Lord, how He used to say, 'John baptized with water, but you shall be baptized with the Holy Spirit" (Acts 11:16). Thus the promised baptism with the Holy Spirit was again fulfilled—and continues to be fulfilled to this day.

On this latter point Peter had earlier declared about "the gift of the Holy Spirit" that "The promise is for you and your children, and for all who are far off, as many as the Lord our God shall call to Himself" (Acts 2:38-39). So to the present day baptism with the Holy Spirit is a continuing promise. So if you have never been filled with the Holy Spirit—if you have made Jesus Lord of your life, you can ask the Lord to fill you with His Spirit.

John knew the importance of the Holy Spirit as He was filled with the Holy Spirit while in his mother's womb. He understood that He was nothing without the Holy Spirit. John also realized that the Holy Spirit is the one that will keep a burning desire in us to keep on seeking the Lord.

*Mat 3:11 Truly, I give baptism with water to those of you whose hearts are changed; but He who comes after me is greater than I, whose shoes I am not good enough to take up: He will give you baptism with the **Holy Spirit** and with fire:*

Receiving the Holy Spirit is not to benefit ourselves. When we receive the Holy Spirit it is to go out and have the power for that what God called you for.

Not one of us can look at the other and say, "I want it the same way He has it"

God is still the Giver of the Holy Spirit and the gifts. And when we receive the Holy Spirit it is to go and do what we are send for. According to the Gospel of Luke, Jesus first said, "You are witnesses of these things" (24:48), and then immediately added, "And behold, I am sending forth the promise of My Father upon you; but you are to stay in the city until you are clothed with power from on high" (24:49). The key word in both Acts and Luke is power; and specifically power for ministry. We can't do anything for ourselves or for God out of our own strength. We need the help, guidance and power of the Holy Spirit for everything we do.

Peter later in Acts says of Jesus that "God anointed Him with the Holy Spirit and with power and . . . He went about doing good, and healing all who were oppressed by the devil" (10:38). This close connection between the Holy Spirit and power for ministry is the basic purpose of baptism (or anointing) with the Holy Spirit.

The anointing or baptism is not always accompanied by signs or manifestations. Some people belief is you don't fall under the anointing you don't receive the Holy Spirit. This is not true. God is not interested in our reactions but in our actions after receiving the Holy Spirit. He is anointing you to go out and make a difference. It could be that there is manifestations, like the speaking of tongues like in Acts 2:4. Here tongues had the purpose of equipping them to go and spread the gospel to all nations. Being filled the Holy Spirit is not a matter of manifestations, but it is a matter of whether your life is changing. If you are filled with the Holy Spirit we need to be changed in becoming more like Jesus. We should be changed and formed into a spirit of holiness.

Often people think the Holy Spirit is only for the preacher or the one who knows enough. The Holy Spirit is for every believer in Jesus Christ. When you accept Him as your Saviour, He promised us the Holy Spirit. Peter's words on the Day of Pentecost about the promise of the gift of the Holy Spirit are preceded by his injunction, "Repent, and let each of you be baptized in the name of Jesus Christ for the forgiveness of your sins, and you shall receive the gift of the Holy Spirit" (Acts 2:38). Only those who belong to Christ can be baptized in the Holy Spirit. The Holy Spirit is part of God and only after someone accepted Jesus can we be filled with the Spirit of God.

Second, recognize and affirm that the promise is a continuing promise. "The promise is for you" (Acts 2:39). You are not dealing with what may be God's will; you are claiming the unfailing promise of God.

Third, pray earnestly. On one occasion Jesus declared, "Ask, and it shall be given to you; seek, and you shall find; knock and it will be opened to you" and thereafter added, *"If you then, being evil, know how to give good gifts to your children, how much more shall your heavenly father give the Holy Spirit to those who ask Him?" (Luke 11:9, 13)*. Are you willing to be earnest and persistent in prayer? The disciples "were continually devoting themselves to prayer" (Acts 1:14) prior to their baptism in the Holy Spirit. How much do you really want this gift of the Holy Spirit?

The laying on of hands is a possible channel for receiving the gift. In several other passages in Acts, hands were laid on prospective recipients: the Samaritans (8:17-18); Saul of Tarsus (9:17); the Ephesians (19:6). You may want to request this ministry from others. To be filled with the Holy Spirit is not only for yourself, but to be equipped to be send out so that we can preach the good news, set the captives free and heal the sick. The more you are obedient and faithful in doing what the Holy Spirit leads you to do, the more you will see the hand of God in your life, your ministry and the life of others. God wants to use each one of us to make a difference.

Many people believe that the Holy Spirit is not needed today. When one speak of the Holy Spirit, people associate being filled with the Spirit with speaking in tongues. Speaking in tongues is one of the manifestations but there is other manifestations of the Holy Spirit too. Being filled with the Holy Spirit is not an option for us as believers it is the power we need to make disciples and therefore we all need to be filled with the Holy Spirit.

In 1 Corinthians 12 Paul writes about the gifts and manifestation of the Holy Spirit.

> ***1Cor 12:1-11*** *Now concerning spiritual gifts, brothers, I do not want you to be uninformed. 2 You know that when you were pagans you were led astray to mute idols, however you were led. 3 Therefore I want you to understand that no one speaking in the Spirit of God ever says "Jesus is accursed!" and no one can say "Jesus is Lord" except in the Holy Spirit.*
> *4 Now there are varieties of gifts, but the same Spirit;*
> *5 and there are varieties of service, but the same Lord;*
> *6 and there are varieties of activities, but it is the same God who empowers them all in everyone.*
> *7 To each is given the manifestation of the Spirit for the common good.*

8 For to one is given through the Spirit the utterance of wisdom, and to another the utterance of knowledge according to the same Spirit,
9 to another faith by the same Spirit, to another gifts of healing by the one Spirit,
10 to another the working of miracles, to another prophecy, to another the ability to distinguish between spirits, to another various kinds of tongues, to another the interpretation of tongues.
11 All these are empowered by one and the same Spirit, who apportions to each one individually as he wills.

Here Paul mentions the following manifestations of the Spirit:

1. Wisdom
2. Knowledge
3. Faith
4. Healing
5. Miracles
6. Prophecy
7. Discernment between spirits
8. Speaking of tongues
9. Interpretation of tongues

Important that Paul writes in verse 11 that it is the same Spirit, and that it is the Spirit who gives to each one individually as He wills. It is not by our holiness or goodness that we deserve the gifts of the Holy Spirit. It is the Holy Spirit that will give as He will. We must remember that these manifestations are for the glory and honor of God. When we are seeking the gifts and manifestations of the Holy Spirit for our own gain, we will not benefit the body of Christ.

There are other lists of gifts in Romans 12:6-8 ("functional" gifts by God's grace) and in Ephesians 4:11-12 ("equipping" gifts from the ascended Christ). However, the list in 1 Corinthians 12:8-10 are specifically "the manifestation of the Holy Spirit" (verse 12). Outside of prophecy (or prophets) which occurs in all three lists, the gifts of the Spirit are uniquely the operation of the Holy Spirit.

The gifts are for the functioning of the body of Christ. And the body needs to function as a whole. Each one is equipped according to what the Holy Spirit gives. You cannot earn the gift by your fleshy works. It is a gift and a promise from the Father, and we should ask the Father to give us the Holy Spirit. The Holy Spirit will then give us the gifts as He thinks needed. The gifts of the Spirit may operate at any time ("distributing to each one individually just as He wills" (1 Cor. 12:11)

Further we must remember it is a gift. And a gift is something you get freely and undeservingly. God is the one that calls people and anoint them to do what He calls them for. When God calls someone, He will empower them through the Holy Spirit to do the work. As soon as you make a mistake, God is not taking your gift away. Paul writes that the calling and the gift is irrevocable. (Rom 11:29) This is just to prove that the working of the Holy Spirit is not dependant on us. He is God and can use anything. God even used a donkey to speak. Therefore let us not become spiritually proud if we operate in the gifts. It is still God's gift and He only blesses us to be a vessel in His hand.

Spiritual gifts are given for the upbuilding of the body of believers: they are "power tools." As the manifestation of the Spirit, they are all supernatural enablements; for example, to speak a word of wisdom, to effectuate healings, to work miracles, to discern various spirits—all for the benefit of others. When the spiritual gifts operate, the Holy Spirit is directly and powerfully on the scene.

An incidental purpose of the gifts is to bring about involvement of all believers. "To each one is given . . . ." Not to a few—such as pastors and teachers—rather each person is to be a channel for some particular manifestation of the Holy Spirit. Everyone is to be actively involved, for the Holy Spirit wishes to manifest Himself not through a few but all.

The spiritual gifts, being totally different from natural capacities, serve to honor God. God, not man, receives all the praise and glory. Today we need the Holy Spirit just as much and even more than the first disciples. We can't afford to do anything if we are not filled by the Spirit of God. It is the Spirit that gives wisdom and understanding, knowledge and insight, might and power and fear of the Lord (Isa 11:2)

Paul writes that to each "is given" not "was given". If the Holy Spirit is no longer in the church at present, then there can be no gifts; but if He is present in power, the gifts are certain to flourish.

The great commission:

He said to them, "Go throughout the whole world and preach the gospel to all people. Whoever believes and is baptized will be saved; whoever does not believe will be condemned. Believers will be given the power to perform miracles: they will drive out demons in my name; they will speak in strange tongues; if they pick up snakes or drink any poison, they will not be harmed; they will place their hands on sick people, and these will get well." (Mark 16:15-18).

When Jesus commissioned His disciples he said that these manifestations of the Holy Spirit WILL follow the believers. The manifestations of the Holy Spirit was not only for the early church it is still for the believer today. If we want to do what Jesus instructed we should be filled with the Holy Spirit and the spiritual gifts will manifest in our ministries, our churches and it will set people free from sin and disease. It is only the Spirit that can do a complete work. Let us allow the Holy Spirit do be fully operative in our lives but also in our ministries.

Chapter 5

Manifestations of the Holy Spirit

*1 Cor 12:7-11 But the manifestation of the Spirit is given to each one for the profit of all: for to one is given the **word of wisdom** through the Spirit to another the **word of knowledge** through the same Spirit, to another **faith** by the same Spirit, to another **gifts of healings** by the same Spirit, to another the **working of miracles**, to another **prophecy**, to another **discerning of spirits**, to another different **kinds of tongues**, to another the **interpretation of tongues**. But one and the same Spirit works all these things, distributing to each one individually as He wills.*

Important to remember: these are manifestations of the Spirit and it's not your natural talents or abilities. These are gifts and manifestations that can't be deserved or purchased. The Spirit is the one that give the manifestation not our own hard work or our being holy.

Act 8:20 *But Peter answered him, "May you and your money go to hell, for thinking that you can buy God's gift with money!*

The Spirit gives and distribute these as He wills. God is not looking for the most holy person to use, he is looking for someone who is willing to be used by Him. God has given you the Holy Spirit, so be available and wiling for Him to use you. He will equip you for the work, He calls you for. He calls the willing not the equipped. Let us now look at the nine manifestations mentioned by Paul:

1. Word of wisdom

This wisdom is not worldly wisdom or knowledge but wisdom that the Holy Spirit gives. Think of Solomon and the wisdom God gave him. Words of wisdom is often about someone's situation, that you in your natural ability could not know. A word of wisdom is used to encourage, give direction and help someone as led by the Holy Spirit.

Example: telling someone not to give up hope because there is a new job opportunity coming. It is the answer to HOW, WHY, WHO, that a person need and just not seem to get the answer.

Examples in bible: Paul (Acts 23:6), Jesus, Solomon

There are three types of wisdom:

- The wisdom of God (I Corinthians 2:6-7)
- The wisdom of the world (I Corinthians 2:6)
- The wisdom of man (Ecclesiastes 1:16-18)

The gift of the word of wisdom is the application of knowledge that God gives you (I Corinthians 2:6-7). This type of wisdom is a gift which cannot be gained through study or experience and should by no means try to replace them. The gift of the word of wisdom is seeing life from God's perspective. As a Christian exercises this gift, he begins to develop a fear of the Lord. This is the *"beginning of wisdom"* according to Proverbs 1:7.

The gift of the word of wisdom is also the revealing of prophetic future; it is speaking hidden truths of what is not known. It is a supernatural perspective to ascertain the divine means for accomplishing God's will in a given situation, and is a divinely given power to appropriate spiritual intuition in problem solving.

Furthermore, this gift involves having a sense of divine direction, being led by the Holy Spirit to act appropriately in a given set of circumstances, and rightly applying knowledge.

The gift of wisdom is the wisdom of God. It is the supernatural impartation of facts; it is not natural. You can't earn it. It is received from God through prayer (Ephesians 1:17).

The Word declares that in Jesus Christ we have wisdom. If you truly want to have the wisdom of God you need to have Jesus. So often people start focussing on the gifts and forget that it is because of Jesus Christ that we have the Holy Spirit. Jesus need to be the centre in all we do and want to do, no matter what it is. Then it will always be done wisely. (1 Cor 1:30 But it is from Him that you have your life in Christ Jesus, Whom God made our Wisdom from God (revealed to us a knowledge of the divine plan of salvation previously hidden, manifesting itself as) our Righteousness—Amplified Bible)

Gen 41:39 And Pharaoh said to Joseph, Seeing that God has made all this clear to you, there is no other man of such wisdom and good sense as you:

Job 28:28 *And he said to man, Truly the fear of the Lord is wisdom, and to keep from evil is the way to knowledge.*

Prov 2:6 For the Lord gives wisdom; out of his mouth come knowledge and reason:

Prov 24:3 The building of a house is by wisdom, and by reason it is made strong:

1 Cor 2:13 *And these are the things which we say, not in the language of man's wisdom, but in words given to us by the Spirit, judging the things of the spirit by the help of the Spirit.*

James 1:5 *But if any man among you is without wisdom, let him make his request to God, who gives freely to all without an unkind word, and it will be given to him.*

James 3:17 *But the wisdom which is from heaven is first holy, then gentle, readily giving way in argument, full of peace and mercy and good works, not doubting, not seeming other than it is.*

2. Word of knowledge

The Word says that God's people perish because of a lack of knowledge.

Hos. 4:6 *My people are destroyed for lack of knowledge: because thou hast rejected knowledge, I will also reject thee, that thou shall be no priest to me: seeing thou hast forgotten the law of thy God, I will also forget thy children.*

A definition according to Webster Dictionary:

Knowledge

1. A clear and certain perception of that which exists, or of truth and fact; the perception of the connection and agreement, or disagreement and repugnancy of our ideas.

We can have no knowledge of that which does not exist. God has a perfect knowledge of all His work. Human knowledge is very limited, and is mostly gained by observation and experience.

Information; power of knowing.

Examples in bible: Noah building the Ark, Elisha knowing that Gehazi lied. A word of knowledge is a definite conviction, impression, or knowing that comes to you in a similitude (a mental picture), a dream, through a vision, or by a Scripture that is quickened to you. It is supernatural insight or understanding of circumstances, situations, problems, or a body of facts by revelation; that is, without assistance by any human resource but solely by divine aid.

Furthermore, the gift of the word of knowledge is revelation of the divine will and plan of God. It involves moral wisdom for right living and relationships, requires objective understanding concerning divine things in human duties, and refers to knowledge of God or of the things that belong to God, as related in the Gospel.

The gifts of the word of wisdom and the word of knowledge function together; knowledge is gained through the Word and a relationship with God and wisdom builds on it. Knowledge given by the Spirit is revelation knowledge and not mere gained knowledge. Revelation knowledge put you to action. When you have revelation knowledge received by the Spirit you will act on this knowledge and it will bring about changes.

When we receive a word of knowledge it will also bring understanding. Knowledge and understanding comes from God. Even Job asked these questions Job 28:12 "But where shall Wisdom be found? and where is the place of understanding? He finds the answer in verse 23 "God understands the way (wisdom) and He knows the place of it.

When we need wisdom, knowledge and understanding we should seek it from God. The more we seek, the more we will find.

3. Discernment of Spirit

Discernment is to be able to recognize what is of God and His Spirit and what is of the flesh and of the devil. Is it necessary to be able to discern? Yes! The Word is warning us that in the last days there will be many spirits and that we need to test the spirits. *1John 4:1 Beloved, believe not every spirit, but try the spirits whether they are of God: because many false prophets are gone out into the world.*

Discerning of spirits is the supernatural ability given by the Holy Spirit to perceive the source of a spiritual manifestation and determine whether it is of God (Acts 10:30-35), of the devil (Acts 16:16-18), of man (Acts 8:18-23), or of the world. It is not mind reading, psychic phenomena, or the ability to criticize and find fault.

Discerning of spirits must be done by the power of the Holy Spirit; He bears witness with our spirit when something is or is not of God. We should not go on our emotions or our feelings. The gift of discerning of spirits is the supernatural power to detect the realm of the spirits and their activities.

It implies the power of spiritual insight—the supernatural revelation of plans and purposes of the enemy and his forces. It is a gift which protects and guards your Christian life.

4. Gift of faith

The gift of faith is operating to perform something impossible by ordinary human efforts. The gift of faith is supernatural, it is when God intervenes with His sovereignty and glory to work a miracle for us. The gift of faith is the supernatural ability to believe God without doubt, combat unbelief, and visualize what God wants to accomplish. It is not only an inner conviction impelled by an urgent and higher calling, but also a supernatural ability to meet adverse circumstances with trust in God's words and messages.

The Bible speaks of several different types of faith which increase from faith to faith (Romans 1:17):

- Saving faith—faith which gets you into Heaven
- (Ephesians 2:8-9)
- Fruit of faith—faith which gets Heaven into you
- (Galatians 5:22-23).
- Gift of faith—stems from saving faith and the fruit of faith; It is the ability to believe for the miraculous (II Thessalonians 1:3).

This gift not only operates in healings and in miracles, but in the realm of the impossible as well. Saving faith produces the active faith of the fruit of the Spirit which, in turn, produces the gift of faith. When the gift of faith is empowered, the results are miraculous! Once again faith is not something you can earn by doing good. Faith comes by hearing the Word of God. (Rom 10:17) The more time we spend in the Word of God the stronger our faith become.

Heb 11:1 Now faith is the substance of things hoped for, the evidence of things not seen.

Faith is to speak the things you cannot see as if it already existing. Although the world don't understand this concept, the spirit is not operating in the fleshy realm but in the unseen. Therefore continue to speak the Word of God and see how your faith grow. The more you have faith the more you will see God's hand moving in your life. **Mat 15:28** *Then Jesus answered her, "O woman, great is your faith! Be it done for you as you desire." And her daughter was healed instantly.*

5. Healing
The gift of healing refers to supernatural healing without human aid; it is a special gift to pray for specific diseases.

Healing can come through the touch of faith (James 5:14-15); by speaking the word of faith (Luke 7:1-10); or by the presence of God being manifested (Mark 6:56; Acts 19:11-12).

The Bible speaks of "gifts" of healing because there are three types of healings: physical (diabetes, blindness, cancer, deafness, etc.), emotional (jealousy, worry, discouragement, and other destructive attitudes), and spiritual (bitterness, greed, and guilt, etc.) healing.

According to Mark 16:17-20, the gifts of healing belong to all believers. You can know whether or not you have the gift of healing by the following:

- By the inner witness of the Holy Spirit (Romans 8:16).
- When you have a special ability to believe for physical healing for someone (Romans 12:3-8).

When you have an overwhelming feeling of compassion which moves you to action (Matthew 20:34).

Healing the sick was one of the instructions Jesus gave to His disciples.

Matt 10:8 Heal the sick, raise the dead, cleanse lepers, cast out demons. You received without paying; give without pay.

Many people are afraid to pray for the sick—what if she is not cured? We must always remember the healing is a manifestation of the Holy Spirit and it is not your ability or your power. As we've read in the previous chapter, Jesus died for our sins and for our healing. Therefore God always wants to heal people, our faith, our obedience and our believing is what stand in Gods way to heal. God is always the same and healing is the one manifestation of the Spirit of God that is still the same. The operation of the gift is not seen in our churches because we don't have the faith to let the healings take place.

If God lays it upon your heart to pray for someone, just be obedient and let the Holy Spirit to the work. It is not your anointing that will bring healing, but the anointing of the Holy Spirit. Healing is the manifestation of the Holy Spirit that is operating through you, it is not your gift or your anointing. Place your trust in the Holy Spirit and forget about your own abilities.

6. Miracles

The definition of miracle according to Webster Dictionary

1. Literally, a wonder or wonderful thing; but appropriately,
2. In theology, an event or effect contrary to the established constitution and course of things, or a deviation from the known laws of nature; a supernatural event. Miracles can be wrought only by Almighty power, as when Christ healed lepers, saying, "I will, be thou clean," or calmed the tempest, "Peace, be still."

A miracle is therefore a supernatural event that could only be done through the supernatural power of the Holy Spirit. A miracle is the performance of something which is against the laws of nature; it is a supernatural power to intervene and counteract earthly and evil forces.

The word *miracles* comes from the Greek word *dunamis* which means "power and might that multiplies itself." The gift of miracles operates closely with the power gifts of faith and healings to bring authority over Satan, sickness, sin, and the binding forces of this age.

Miracles can also be defined as supernatural intercessions of God. God exhorts us with energy to do something that is not natural or normal to us. Just as the ministry gift of miracles is the expression of prayer, so is the function of the Holy Spirit to direct our prayers (Romans 8:26).

In the Word there are many examples of miracles done through the power of God. The creating of the universe alone is a miracle. The Israelites survival and provision in the desert, the miracles done by the prophets and the most important the birth of our Saviour, Jesus Christ. In the New Testament it starts with the miracles by Jesus, following the miracles done by the disciples and continues with the miracles done by Christians. Miracles were not only for the early church, it is still for us today.

Jesus said, *"Ye do err, not knowing the scriptures, nor the power of God"* (Matthew 22:29). The Apostle Paul warned Timothy about those who have a form of godliness, but deny the power thereof, and he told him not to associate with such people (II Timothy 3:5). If you want the gift of miracles to operate in you, make sure that the Word of God is in you and that you are being influenced by the right people. Miracles are the product of the spoken Word of God, because the Word of God and God are one (Psalm 33:6).

Once again we see that the gift of miracles is a manifestation of the Spirit and that we need to know the Word and have a relationship with God to operate in these gifts.

7. Prophecy

The gift of prophecy edifies, exhorts, and comforts (I Corinthians 14:3); helps us build up or strengthen; and should lead us to the Word of God. It is the ministry of the Holy Spirit to convict of sin, of righteousness, and of judgment to come (John 16:8-11).

Prophecy is divinely inspired and anointed utterance; a supernatural proclamation in a known language. It is the manifestation of the Spirit of God—not of intellect (I Corinthians 12:7), and it may be possessed and operated by all who have the infilling of the Holy Spirit (I Corinthians 14:31)

The gift of prophecy operates when there is high worship (I Samuel 10:5-6), when others prophets are present (I Samuel 10:9-10), and when hands are laid on you by ministers (Acts 19:1-6).

The gift of prophecy (I Corinthians 12) and the office of the prophet (Ephesians 4:11) are not the same thing.

There is a ministry of the prophet, but not everyone is a prophet. For example, a boy may wear a Cubs baseball cap, but that does not mean he plays professional baseball for the Chicago Cubs. You may prophesy, but operating in the simple gift of prophecy does not qualify you to stand in the office of a prophet, much like wearing a jersey of a professional team does not qualify you to play for that team—you must be gifted. To stand in the office of a prophet, one must have a consistent manifestation of at least two of the revelation gifts (*word of wisdom, word of knowledge,* or *discerning of spirits*) plus prophecy.

Prophecy is not the intepretation of tongues.

The Bible says that *"greater is he that prophesieth than he that speaketh with tongues"* (I Corinthians 14:5), even though both are inspired utterances. Tongues, of course, is inspired utterance in an "unknown" tongue. The interpretation of tongues is inspired utterance telling that which was spoken in tongues. Prophecy, on the other hand, is inspired utterance in a "known" tongue. The difference between interpretation and prophecy is that interpretation is dependent upon tongues, whereas prophecy is not.

Prophecy is not prediction.

People sometimes think that "prophecy" means to predict (foretell) what will happen in the future. Actually, the simple gift of prophecy is essentially forthtelling; it is a ministry to make people better and more useful Christians now. Prophecy in the New Testament church carries no prediction with it whatsoever, for *"he that prophesieth speaketh unto men to edification, and exhortation, and comfort"* (I Corinthians 14:3). Notice that there is no mention of the word *prediction* here.

Prophecy is not the same thing as preaching.

The words *preach* and *prophesy* come from two entirely different Greek words. To "preach" means to proclaim, announce, cry, or tell. Jesus said, *"Go ye into all the world, and PREACH the gospel."* (Mark 16:15). Note that He didn't say to prophesy the Gospel.

The word *prophecy* means to "bubble up, to flow forth, or to cause to drop like rain." Teaching and preaching are preplanned, but prophecy is not.

The Bible tells us that we are to *"Despise not prophesyings. Prove all things."* I Thessalonians 5:20-21. When a prophecy is given, we are to test it and hold on to what is good in it.

It is important to know that not all words of "prophecy" is inspired by the Holy Spirit. Therefore discernment is so important. The Word teaches us on how to judge prophecy. Let us look at these guidelines in the Word.

i) A prophet shall be know by his/her fruit (Matt 7:16-20)
ii) Is Jesus glorified, He is the greatest prophecy (Rev. 19:10 For the testimony of Jesus is the spirit of prophecy)
iii) Is the prophecy in line with the Word of God (Num 23:19 God is not man, that he should lie, or a son of man, that he should change his mind. Has he said, and will he not do it? Or has he spoken, and will he not fulfill it?)
iv) Pray and ask God if the prophecy is in His will for your life.

8. Speaking in tongues

Speaking in tongues is a supernatural utterance through the power of the Holy Spirit in a person that manifests as spiritual language. The spiritual language is not for the understanding of others. (1 Cor 14: 2) Speaking in a spiritual tongue is communication with the Spirit. The Holy Spirit energizes the tongue to edification of oneself.

Diverse tongues is the most misunderstood and dynamic gift. It is not your prayer language, but it can surface through intercession, conference, or through the individual. Supernatural utterance in languages not known to the speaker; these languages may be existent in the world, revived from some past culture, or "unknown" in the sense that they are a means of communication inspired by the Holy Spirit (Isaiah 28:11; Mark 16:17; Acts 2:4, 10:44-48, 19:1-7; I Corinthians 12:10, 13:1-3, 14:2, 4-22, 26-32).

The spiritual gift involving ability to speak in foreign language(s) not previously studied or to respond to experience of the Holy Spirit by uttering sounds which those without the gift of interpretation could not understand. At Pentecost the church received the gift to communicate the gospel in foreign languages (Acts 2). God gave His Spirit to all His people to empower them to witness and prophesy. In Corinth some members of the church uttered sounds the rest of the congregation did not understand (I Corinthians 12-14). This led to controversy and division. Paul tried to unite the church, assuring the church that there are different gifts but only one Spirit (I Corinthians 12:4-11).

There are three types of tongues mentioned in the Bible:

	Three Types of Tongues
1.	An unknown tongue unto God (I Corinthians 14:2). This type of tongue edifies you (I Corinthians 14:4; Jude 20), assists you in prayer (Romans 8:26-27), stirs up the prophetic ministry (I Corinthians 14:5), refreshes your soul (Isaiah 28:11-12), gives victory over the devil (Ephesians 6:18), and helps you worship in the Spirit (I Corinthians 14:14-15; Hebrews 2:12). When you sing in the Spirit, God joins in with you and confuses and defeats the enemy (Isaiah 30:29-31); it breaks the yoke of bondage (Acts 16:25); it brings you into the presence of God (Psalm 22:3); and it aids you in intercession (Romans 8:26).
2.	A known tongue that is a sign to unbelievers. (I Corinthians 14:2; Acts 2:6).
3.	A tongue that is understood through *interpretation* and edifies the church (I Corinthians 14:15).

9. Interpretation of tongues

Interpretation of tongues is a supernatural verbalization and subsequent interpretation to reveal the meaning of a diverse tongue. This gift operates out of the mind of the Spirit rather than out of the mind of man.

It is important to note that "interpretation" of tongues is not the same thing as "translation" of tongues, for the interpreter never understands the tongue he or she is interpreting. For example, the message in tongues may be long and the interpretation short because the interpretation only gives the meaning. On the other hand, one may speak a short time in tongues and then given a lengthy interpretation. Yet still, at other times, the interpretation is almost word for word.

The Word of God says that if you pray in tongues, you should pray that you will also interpret—not only for the benefit of others—but for your own benefit as well.

If someone speaks in tongues, you can ask God to move through you to give the interpretation so others will understand, but you can also do this in your private prayers for your own personal benefit. You can pray, "Father, help me understand what I've just said to you in the Spirit," and the Lord will give you the interpretation.

Once again I want to remind you that it is all about the Holy Spirit and God's Kingdom. On one of our visits to Israel, while worshipping in the Upper room, I started speaking in another tongue. Next to me were standing a Russian couple, the next moment they started responding to my talking, although I didn't understand anything they said, they understood the tongue I was speaking in and were filled with the Holy Spirit.

Looking at these nine gifts of the Holy Spirit

1) Word of wisdom
2) Word of knowledge
3) Prophecy
4) Discernment
5) Faith
6) Healing
7) Miracles
8) Speaking of tongues
9) Interpretation of tongues

the most important thing is to remember that these are manifestations of the Holy Spirit. It has nothing to do with our abilities or our status. It is all about our Father and His Kingdom, giving all the glory to Jesus Christ.

If you are filled with the Holy Spirit and serve God with a pure heart, He will certainly use you for His Kingdom.

Chapter 6

Fruit of the Spirit

Galatians 5:22 "The fruit of the spirit is love, joy, peace, patience, kindness, goodness, faithfulness, gentleness, self-control."

There are nine fruits of the Spirit mentioned. These fruits are the products of being filled with the Holy Spirit and living a Spirit filled life. The fruits are not a choice we have—to do or not to do. The fruit is the work of the presence of the Holy Spirit within us. Just as a apple tree bears apples, when you are filled with Holy Spirit you should bear fruit of the Spirit.

The fruit is not for ourselves, but for others seeing us, and living around us. Just like an apple tree look attractive when it is full in bloom, the apples will become rotten and eventually fall under the tree if they are not eaten. The same with our fruit. The fruit is there for others to come and eat off. Our fruit is their to bring love, joy and peace to others.

As children of God, we are trees of righteousness that have been planted by the Lord to produce fruit. The fruit we need to produce is the fruit of the Spirit.

Isaiah 61:3 "That they might be called trees of righteousness, the planting of the LORD, that he might be glorified."

Psalm 92:13 "Those that be planted in the house of the LORD shall flourish in the courts of our God."

By our fruit we will be known—Mat 12:33 "To have good fruit you must have a healthy tree; if you have a poor tree, you will have bad fruit. A tree is known by the kind of fruit it bears. Mat 7:20 Wherefore by their fruits you shall know them. Jesus said to the disciplines that we will know the false prophets by their fruit. So ask yourself, what is my fruit? What do others see when I'm not ministering or are just at home? The struggle is ongoing, between flesh and spirit. But we need to get to that point where our fleshy desires are not dominant and that our behaviour, our thoughts and our talk are directed and lead by the Holy Spirit. "the flesh sets its desire against the Spirit, and the Spirit against the flesh; for these are in opposition to one another" (Gal.5: 15-17). There is victory, however: "If we live by the Spirit, let us also walk by the Spirit" (Gal. 5:25).

When a new tree is planted it doesn't immediately bear fruit. It takes time to grow and it takes time to bear bigger en better fruit. A tree needs pruning and attention to develop into the best tree it can be. The same with us. The moment we accept Jesus Christ as our Saviour we become part of a bigger garden, God's Kingdom. The salvation is instant but maturing as a child of God is a process. Then we need the Holy Spirit to guide and teach us. The Holy Spirit is like the Water that gives us life. The more we drink of the Water, the better we grow, the stronger we become.

John 4:14 But whoever takes a drink of the water that I will give him shall never, no never be thirsty any more. But the water that I will give him shall become a spring of water welling up within him unto eternal life.

The pruning we need to grow is not suffering and tormenting. The Word of God is the scissors that are pruning us. *John 15:2 (Ampl) Any branch in Me that does not bear fruit (that stops bearing) He cuts away (trims off, takes away); and He cleanses and repeatedly prunes every branch that onitnues to bear fruit, to make it bear more and richer and more excellent fruit. 3 Your are cleansed and pruned already,* **because of the word** *which I have given you.*

This emphasize once again the importance to spend time in the Word and to know the Word of God. The Word is our mirror (James 1:22-26) and the Word will reveal to us our strengths and that what we need to change. To bear fruit on your own is not possible.

* **First we need to be rooted in Christ Jesus**. *Isa 11:10 And in that day there shall be a root of Jesse, which shall stand for an ensign of the people; to it shall the Gentiles seek: and his rest shall be glorious.*
* **Be filled with the Holy Spirit**, our Counselor and Teacher (Luk 12:12; 1 John 2:27; *Joh 14:26 But the Helper, the Holy Spirit, whom the Father will send in my name, he will teach you all things and bring to your remembrance all that I have said to you.*
* **Study the Word** *Mat 4:4 But he answered, "It is written, "'Man shall not live by bread alone, but by every word that comes from the mouth of God.'"*
* **Apply the Word in your life** *Heb 4:12 For the word of God is living and active, sharper than any two-edged sword, piercing to the division of soul and of spirit, of joints and of marrow, and discerning the thoughts and intentions of the heart. Heb 4:12 For the word of God is living and active, sharper than any two-edged sword, piercing to the division of soul and of spirit, of joints and of marrow, and discerning the thoughts and intentions of the heart.*

There is so much power in the Word of God! God created the whole earth through His Word. Jesus was conceived by only a Word, and Jesus is the Word. John 1:1 In the beginning (before all time) was the Word (Christ) and the Word was with god, and the Word was God Himself. No matter what situation you are in or are facing, the Word has an answer. We just need to apply this Word to our life and we will see changes. God's Word can create, can heal, can supply and can protect. No matter what you need it is all in God's Word. The choice is yours, if you are going to make use of the power given to you! Start by writing down scriptures and memorising them. Declare the Word in your life, and you will see how the power of the Word and the Holy Spirit bring about the change!

We need both the operation of the gifts and the maturation of the fruits for a Spirit filled Christian life.

The nine fruits of the Spirit are:

- love
- joy (gladness)
- peace
- patience (an even temper, forbearance)
- kindness
- goodness (benevolence)
- faithfulness
- gentleness (meekness, humility)
- self-control (self-restraint, continence)

When our spirit is filled with the Spirit of God, we will start bearing God's fruit. The world function differently than God's Kingdom and therefore if we are Spirit filled the world will see a difference in our behaviour.

- In times of fear—we must produce love
- In times of mourning and sadness—we must produce joy.
- In times of storm—we must produce peace.
- In times of impatience—we must produce patience.
- In times of aggression—we must produce gentleness.
- In times of evil—we must produce goodness.
- In times of doubt—we must produce faith and faithfulness.
- In times of pride—we must produce meekness.
- In times of over-indulgence—we must produce temperance.

To bear fruit we need to stay rooted in Christ and filled with the Holy Spirit and the Word. The fruit is the fruit of the Spirit and not the fruit of our own efforts. The more we bear fruit the more lives will be touched and changed by our fruit. Once again it is not possible to bear fruits of the spirit out of our own fleshy will. What this means is that these fruit are qualities of God. When we are rooted in Christ, filled with the Spirit of the Lord we start to be like Him. Do you realize that this is not the same as the world? We need to acknowledge our own weakness and worldly desires, confess them and ask the Holy Spirit to help us. It is not by might or by power but only by His Spirit that we can change. (Zec. 4:6)

The first fruit mentioned is **love**. Love is the beginning of all the gifts. God is love, and if we want to bear His fruit, the first thing we'll need to share with others is love. Love has different words in Greek. The love that is mentioned here is the "agape" love. Agape means the love that God has for mankind. When reading 1 Cor. 13, we realize that if we don't have love, we have nothing. It is because God so loved the world that He send us His only Son, Jesus. (John 3:16). Loving others like God loves us, will only be possible through His Spirit. When His love is imparted into us, only then will we be able to love like He love us. Loving others is therefore the one thing we should all strife to. If you love someone, the way God intended us to love one another, the rest of the fruit will also become visible in our lives. Jesus prayed that the same love that God the Father has would be in you. *"And I have declared to them Your name, and will declare it, that the love with which You loved Me may be in them, and I in them." (John 17:26)*

Joy as a fruit of the spirit is not only happiness, but a lasting gladness. Happiness is something that comes and go. In the world people often feel happy when something happen, but as soon as their circumstances changes, their happiness changes. Joy is not only a fruit it is also a strength.

And do not be grieved, for the joy of the LORD is your strength." Neh. 8:10

This joy is something we only experience if the Lord is our Strength.

Definition of JOY, *(Websters Dictionary).*

- The passion or emotion excited by the acquisition or expectation of good; that excitement of pleasurable feelings which is caused by success, good fortune, the gratification of desire or some good possessed, or by a rational prospect of possessing what we love or desire; gladness; exultation; exhilaration of spirits.
- Joy is a delight of the mind, from the consideration of the present or assured approaching possession of a good.
- Happiness; felicity.
- A glorious and triumphant state.

Joy is therefore something we all need to cope in the world we live in. It is only if we have God's joy in our spirit that we will be able to keep hope and be positive. God never changes and if everything around us changes and fail, we can be certain that the joy of the Lord is our strength.

The fruit of peace is not the absence of war, it is much more. Once again remind yourself of the Shalom peace we've spoken about earlier. God's peace is not dependant on our surroundings, and therefore when we have God's peace we will be calm in every storm. No matter what happen around us, it could affect our emotions but not change who we are in Christ. It is only with God's peace that we can experience peace in all circumstances.

Patience is something we need not only in the world but also in our walk with God. Throughout the Word we see that people that were patient, all got the reward. Noah, Abraham, Joseph and even David are a few examples of people who had to be patient to do or experience what God said.

But as for that seed in the good soil, these are the people who, hearing the Word, hold it fast in a just, noble, virtuous and worthy heart, and steadily bring forth fruit with **patience**. *(Luk 8:15 Ampl)*

The lack of patience is the one thing that keeps many people from entering their destiny. Our timing is not God's timing and if we learn to focus on God's Word and His promises with patience, we will see His promises fulfilled. To live in the fullness of God includes to have His patience.

Kindness is to many people a option. It is easy to be kind to the people we love and care for. But the fruit of kindness is to be kind even to those who is hurting and disappointing you. Jesus is the perfect example we have of kindness. He was kind to sinners, the sick and even those who crucified Him.

Luk 6:35 *But love your enemies, and do good, and lend, expecting nothing in return, and your reward will be great, and you will be sons of the Most High, for he is **kind** to the ungrateful and the evil.*

Kindness is not only the fruit of the Spirit but something that God instruct us as His children to be.

Epeh 4:32 *Be kind to one another, tenderhearted, forgiving one another, as God in Christ forgave you.*

Goodness comes from God. He shared all His goodness with His children.

Exo 33:19 *And He said, "I will make all my goodness pass before you and will proclaim before you My name 'The LORD.' And I will be gracious to whom I will be gracious, and will show mercy on whom I will show mercy.*

Jer 31:14 *I will feast the soul of the priests with abundance, and my people shall be satisfied with my goodness, declares the LORD."*

We can only give what we have. We received all the goodness to satisfy ourselves from the Lord. Therefore doing good to others is not something we should consider it should be something we do on a daily basis. The more we are sharing goodness, the more goodness and mercy will follow us all the days of our lives.

Faithfulness means to be loyal, dependable and do keep your promise and your word. The Word says, let our yes be our yes and our no be our no.

James 5:12 But above all, my brothers, do not swear, either by heaven or by earth or by any other oath, but let your "yes" be yes and your "no" be no, so that you may not fall under condemnation.

In society today it is so easy to say you will do something, make a vow or a promise and then just not to keep it or do it. Keep your promises and being loyal is a fruit of the Spirit. God always keep His promises and never let us down.

2Co 1:20 For all the promises of God find their Yes in him. That is why it is through him that we utter our Amen to God for his glory.

Gentleness is the gentle, mild and kind manner that we treat others. Gentleness is a fruit that once again Jesus is our perfect example. If we think how He handled the prostitutes and sinners, we can see that His gentle manner of addressing issues brought healing. A gentle word is like healing.

Gentleness is a quality that a harsh and sinful world is desperately in need off.

We all have some situations in our lives that we find challenging and that we need to let go off. When we look at the fruit of the flesh one of the counterfeits for them will be **self-control.** This is one of the fruit of the Spirit that most people try to achieve on their own. The moment we realize that on my own and with my own abilities I am not able to do good, then only can we bear the fruit of self-control.

The Word says we can do all things, only it is not through my own strength but through Christ in me. *Phil. 4:13 I have strength for all things in Christ Who empowers me.*

If you are struggling with self-control, remember it is a fruit of the Spirit, it is not your self-control, it is His. The more you focus on Jesus and be filled with the Holy Spirit, the more you will have self-control.

So often people try to eat less, stop smoking or drinking, be more active, work better. What ever you have tried in the past and not succeeding, submit it unto the Lord and ask the Holy Spirit to help you to bear more fruit. Self-control is a fruit that will grow as we let the Word prune us and the Holy Spirit teach us.

One way in which the enemy comes and steal our fruit is through fear. Fear is not from God. Jesus overcame fear so that we can live in victory.

2Tim 1:7 for God gave us a spirit not of fear but of power and love and self-control.

Fear comes and take away love, power and self-control. It is clear that the enemy know the importance of bearing fruit. He cannot attack the Spirit of the Lord, so then he try to stop us from bearing fruit. The enemy bring fear through circumstances and challenges. The moment we fear, we take our eyes of Jesus and start looking to the circumstances. Think of the Israelites that had to keep their eyes on the snake (proto type of Jesus) in the desert, and Peter when walking on the water. The moment we fear, that what we fear, will come upon us. Job 3:25 For the thing that I fear comes upon me, and what I dread befalls me.

We don't have to fear anything. All power and principalities are under the feet of Jesus who overcame the enemy on the cross. If you are struggling with fear in your life, write down these scriptures, memorise them and declare them over your life. The word is active and alive (Hebr 4:12) Ask the Holy Spirit to help you to take self-control and to cancel all fear in your life by confessing these verses.

Gen 15:1 After these things the word of the LORD came to Abram in a vision: "Fear not, Abram, I am your shield; your reward shall be very great."

Deut 3:22 You shall not fear them, for it is the LORD your God who fights for you.'

Jos 8:1 *And the LORD said to Joshua, "Do not fear and do not be dismayed*

Deut 31:6 Be strong and courageous. Do not fear or be in dread of them, for it is the LORD your God who goes with you. He will not leave you or forsake you."

Judge 6:23 But the LORD said to him, "Peace be to you. Do not fear; you shall not die."

Ps 23:4 Even though I walk through the valley of the shadow of death, I will fear no evil, for you are with me; your rod and your staff, they comfort me.

Ps 91:5 You will not fear the terror of the night, nor the arrow that flies by day,

Ps 118:6 The LORD is on my side; I will not fear. What can man do to me?

Matt 10:31 Fear not, therefore; you are of more value than many sparrows.

Matt 17:7 But Jesus came and touched them, saying, "Rise, and have no fear."

Luk 8:50 But Jesus on hearing this answered him, "Do not fear; only believe, and she will be well."

Luk 12:32 "Fear not, little flock, for it is your Father's good pleasure to give you the kingdom.

Rom 8:15 For you did not receive the spirit of slavery to fall back into fear, but you have received the Spirit of adoption as sons, by whom we cry, "Abba! Father!"

2Tim 1:7 for God gave us a spirit not of fear but of power and love and self-control.

Heb 13:6 So we can confidently say, "The Lord is my helper; I will not fear; what can man do to me?"

1Pet 3:14 But even if you should suffer for righteousness' sake, you will be blessed. Have no fear of them, nor be troubled,

1John 4:18 There is no fear in love, but perfect love casts out fear. For fear has to do with punishment, and whoever fears has not been perfected in love.

When we look at these nine fruit of the Spirit we see that they are all very important in changing and transforming our lives. We must remember that they are there to touch the lives of those around us and help us to get people to meet our Saviour, Jesus Christ.

We should always remember that it is all about the Lord, and His Kingdom! We are only the branches bearing fruit through Jesus as the root and the Holy Spirit as the Helper.

Chapter 7

The Fullness of life

Col 2:10 (Ampl) And you are in Him, made full and having come to fullness of life (in Christ you too are filled with the Godhead-Father, Son and Holy Spirit—and reach full spiritual stature). And He is the Head of all rule and authority (of every angelic principality and power).

This is such a powerful verse in the Bible. It says that once you accept Jesus Christ as your Saviour, you are filled with the Godhead and have come to FULLNESS of life. Ask yourself am I living a life of fullness? So many Christians believe that a life of fullness is not possible, but according to God's Word it is not only possible, but a reality. Every child of God has the privilege to live a life of fullness. Do you realise who you are in Christ?

Through Jesus Christ we can have a life of fullness. *John 1:16 For out of His fullness (abundance) we have all received (all had a share and we were all supplied with) one grace after another and spiritual blessing upon spiritual blessing and even favor upon favor and gift heaped upon gift.*

This means that everything you need, all grace, gifts, blessings and favour is already yours. It says **"we have all received"** meaning it has already been done! You have received the grace you need to overcome every challenge. You have received all the spiritual blessings to be a blessing to others. You have received favor like Joseph to be what God called you to be and you have received every gift to fulfil the calling God placed on your life. There is no excuse to not live a life of abundance and fullness. The key is to be rooted in Christ and that He always stay the centre of your life. The fullness is in Him, not in our abilities or our efforts. *Eph 1:23 Which is His body, the fullness of Him Who fills all in all (for in that body lives the full measure of Him Who makes everything complete, and Who fills everything everywhere with Himself)*

This means that in order to live a life of fullness we have to live a Spirit filled life. Where the Spirit is there is liberty and fullness. The Lord promised that whenever we accept Jesus, He will give us the Holy Spirit.

Luk 11:13 If you then, who are evil, know how to give good gifts to your children, how much more will the heavenly Father give the Holy Spirit to those who ask him!"

To receive the Holy Spirit is not something you can work for. We can never deserve the Holy Spirit. We have to ask our Father, He will give it to us.

Read, study and apply the Word in your life. The more you will spend time to read and study the Word, the more your life will be filled with the Fullness of God. Jesus is the Word and He is our Fullness.

The more we get to know the Word and be changed to be like Jesus, the more we will have an intimate relationship with the Lord as Abba Father. Just as a child longing for his parents, so we need to long for our Father. The more we miss Him, the more we will seek Him, the more we will find Him.

In Him we have everything and lack nothing. You will get to know God in every area of your life and will experience the fullness of the Lord as the Father, the Son and the Spirit in your life.

If you have desired a life of fullness—start having a relationship with the Lord of Fullness today! Your life will never be the same.

In conclusion I pray,

- that you will always turn to the Lord and call on His name;
- that Jesus Christ will be your Saviour and that you will believe in Him as the Complete Sacrifice;
- that you will get to know the Lord as your loving and caring Abba Father;
- that you will be filled with the Holy Spirit and live a life that bear much fruit;

then your life will be filled with the fullness of God.

CPSIA information can be obtained
at www.ICGtesting.com
Printed in the USA
LVHW102258081121
702820LV00015B/953